Time to Tell 'Em Off!

Time to Tell 'Em Off!

A Pocket Guide to Overcoming

Peer Ridicule

Deanna Miller

http://www.booklocker.com/bookpages/dmiller.html

Published 2002

Cover design by Andria Miller, Cathi Stevenson, and Deanna Miller

Formatting assistance from JagTek
Photo scanning and book printing by Balmar Printing & Graphics

Manufactured in the United States of America

Booklocker.com, Inc.
2002

For the children and teenagers who
suffer abuse from their peers.

Always remember God loves you,
and other people cannot take away
your worth in His eyes.

Table of Contents

Time to Tell 'Em Off!

Chapter 1
Who Is This Book For?

Kids who pick on other kids are committing a crime. They are robbing others of their confidence, self-esteem, peace of mind, and sense of security. Plus they're having a great time doing it. So if you happen to be one of these criminals and you thought it would be funny to open up this book, keep in mind that I'm laughing at you from the other end. You need some serious help, you don't even know it, and I'm not going to give it to you.

What I'm talking about here is not the harmless teasing that just about everybody does to friends or family at some point. I'm talking about the nasty jeering that goes on in elementary, middle, and even high schools so often that most adults just shrug it off as part of growing up. Kids, too, act like it's no big deal. But when you are the target of the ridicule, you know it is a very big deal.

If your peers are making fun of you and you'd like some help, I sympathize with you. I understand how you feel. I was ridiculed myself off and on from kindergarten through ninth grade, and sometimes I still fantasize about smacking around those idiots, or at least telling them off. But I'm an adult now. It's too late for me to stand up to the bullies of my youth.

However, it's not too late for you to take back the magic of childhood and adolescence that should be yours. That's why I've written this book for you.

Chapter 2
Why Me? The Reasons Kids Make Fun of You

Being ridiculed is a very upsetting experience. Your heart beats fast as if to tell you your body is ready to run from the attack. You feel hurt and angry, but the anger is frustrating and useless because you are too afraid of what the bullies will do if you use your anger to defend yourself. This fear is understandable because most likely you are outnumbered. If you hardly know your attackers and you had a fairly good self-image before they started picking you apart, you also feel bewildered. They don't even know you. You've done nothing to them. Why should they hate you?

Inevitably you ask yourself, "Why me? What is so wrong with me that I deserve this terrible treatment?" Then you come up with a list of all your flaws, usually many of them physical. After obsessing over these flaws for a while, you conclude that you're worthless.

Hold on right there! When a person is robbed, does he think, "Oh, this happened to me because I'm such a lowly, unimportant person and the thief is so much better than I am"? No way does he think that, and neither should you. As I said before, being picked on is the same as being robbed. Whether it's your money or your self-confidence they're stealing, you're still dealing with low-life thugs.

So let me assure you now: there is nothing wrong with you. You may protest, "But you don't know how fat I am" or "You haven't seen how ugly I look with my braces." Well, without even knowing you, I'm still certain there is nothing wrong with you. There is only what you *believe* to be wrong with you. That said, let's take a look at what the bullies may *believe* to be wrong with you...and what is actually wrong with *them*.

The Way You Look

Each person looks different in some way from everyone else. This difference is good. It makes you unique, an original creation not exactly like any other in the world.

Unfortunately, in the social war zone of school, many of us would welcome the camouflage of sameness to avoid being attacked. The lucky kids who grow smoothly—whose noses, for example, don't grow before their faces do—are able to fit in by wearing the right clothes. Sometimes the right clothes are the ones that everybody else is wearing. Sometimes the right clothes are the ones that rebel in a cool way against what other people are wearing. Whichever the case, some kids are protected from attack because nothing about them stands out enough for the bullies to take notice.

However, if your appearance does not blend into the crowd, it is possible that the kids who are socially immature will point out and laugh about your differences. Notice that I say differences, not flaws. Please do not let them trick you into believing that your differences are flaws. If you do, you're letting the thieves steal your stuff. Kids may judge you to be too large, too skinny, too tall, too short, or too whatever. Maybe they decide they are bothered by your glasses, your braces, your skin color, your face, your body...who knows? The point is you don't look ordinary to them.

Well, congratulations! You also don't look plain and boring. Perhaps you even stand out because you are good-looking. I'm not kidding! Whether attractive people become part of the popular crowd or social outcasts depends mostly on how they act, not how they look. The same goes for people who are not thought of as physically attractive. If you don't believe me, answer this: Have you ever seen a popular cheerleader who was—how can I put it?—not thin and not pretty?

I've seen several.

The Way You Act

In my experience, the way you act has much more to do with why you are being picked on than how you look. This is good news because there are some things about the way you look that you just can't change, but you *can* change the way you act!

I know this may be hard for you to face, but people who are ridiculed usually act insecure—even before the attacks start. When you act unsure of yourself, it's like letting the robbers know that you're nervous because you don't have a home security system. You're showing them that you are vulnerable and that, if they pick on you, they will hurt you. You're giving off the message that you believe you're not as good (worthy, smart, attractive, whatever) as they are. Even if you are just as good as—or better than—they are, if you don't believe it, why should they? They would much rather believe that they are better than you. This makes them feel good. It's the sad truth about human nature.

People don't like to see others who are smarter, cuter, richer, happier, more talented, or better off than they are in any way. They like to find or imagine things that are wrong with other people to make themselves feel better. Just look at the success of the tabloids. These magazines are constantly telling us one message: the stars may be rich, beautiful, and famous, but they're not better off than you are! They're addicted to drugs and alcohol. They're going through painful divorces. They're battling deadly diseases. They're getting older. They're gaining weight. They were kidnapped by aliens and have been doing bad movies ever since.

The kids who make fun of you are the same people who will someday buy these magazines to feel better about their sad lives.

Real-Life Examples:
The Link Between Ridicule and the Way You Look and Act

Let me give you some real-life examples of how the way you look and act can affect the way others treat you.

When I was in kindergarten, before anyone started picking on me, I was a cute kid. The awkward stage hadn't set in yet, and I was pretty. I didn't think I was pretty, though. I also felt nervous around the other kids, so I acted very shy. There was a girl on my school bus who was not pretty at all, but she started to make fun of me, calling me ugly every day. At the time I couldn't understand why she was treating me so badly. Now I know that she must have been jealous of me because I was cute. So how could an unattractive person get away with picking on an attractive person? Well, I acted so shy that she realized she could easily put me down and raise herself up. She was right.

Things got worse for me after that. During my pre-teen and early teenage years, my body and face grew in the most awkward way. I got very tall and very thin, without any curves at all. If I'd been a plant, I would have been a stem without any flowers or even any leaves. My cute little nose grew big, but the rest of my face stayed practically as skinny as my long giraffe neck. Luckily, I still had nice eyes, but by fifth grade these last good features were hidden behind the glare of large, square glasses.

A week before the beginning of seventh grade, my orthodontist put the final touches on my embarrassing looks by cementing braces to every tooth I had. The worst part of it was the "palatal expanding device" he put across the roof of my mouth. The "palatal expanding device" was a metal bar that basically widened my upper jaw while narrowing my circle of friends. The bar got in the way of talking and eating. It made me talk funny. It made me rush to the restroom after each meal to brush my teeth and remove the food stuck between the bar and the roof of my mouth. I had to wear the bar for a whole miserable year, during which time I avoided talking. The braces didn't come off until just before ninth grade.

Of course, it was easy for kids to make fun of me all through those years because I agreed that I was ugly, and I felt terrible about myself. Kids even picked on me for features that hadn't occurred to me to feel self-conscious about. For example, two older boys I didn't know (and who were *not* good-looking themselves) yelled out, "Seen the ghost?" and laughed and pointed at me every time they passed me in the hallways. That was how I realized that I had very fair skin. It seemed like everyone thought there was something wrong with me. I became more and more shy and unfriendly because I assumed nobody liked me, and I focused all my attention on my studies, where I excelled.

I thought the mockery would stop when I started high school. My braces were taken off to reveal lovely, straight teeth, and my glasses were replaced with contacts. My face and body were starting to fill out, too. I was definitely beginning to look pretty again. But the irony was that the worst ridicule of all was still ahead of me.

Throughout middle school—and even some time before that, I think—my siblings and I had been the target of ridicule by a group of obnoxious, mostly older boys who sat at the back of our school bus. Every day during our ride home, our ears would prickle as we heard our names yelled out by these boys in mocking tones. They said nasty things about us and threw chalk at us.

As always, the abuse puzzled and angered me. These jerks didn't even know us. They weren't in any of my classes. Heck, they weren't even in my grade! Plus they were not good-looking and not intelligent. They were the types who barely passed. They didn't have anything to brag about themselves, so how could they dare to put anyone else down?

Well, my siblings and I were all quiet and studious. Also, in their opinion, we were goody-goodies. But the main reason they targeted us was because we were meek. We hardly ever tried to defend ourselves, and no one else—including the bus driver—told them to stop, so they got away with making fun of us. By ninth grade they were still harassing us on the bus, but unlike in past years, that year several of them also turned up in one of my classes.

I was in honors classes for all subjects except math. My math class was a combination of freshmen who were at the average math level and upper-classmen who were at the below-average level. So that's how I got stuck with the older boys from the bus. Added to that was another longtime enemy: one of the "Seen the ghost?" guys. The rest of my classmates probably would not have made fun of me ordinarily, but in that bizarre situation, where the older boys were so bold in their persecution of me and yet went unpunished, everyone else felt encouraged to join in, or at least to laugh.

What happened to me in that classroom each day was madness. I sat hunched over in my assigned seat in the middle of the room, wishing—practically praying—I could disappear, while insults came from in front, behind, and either side of me. Basically, all the kids in the class entertained themselves the entire period by ridiculing me. The teacher was an old lady who must have been losing her hearing and her sight because, to my disbelief, she never once tried to discipline the kids when they spoke out of turn to humiliate me. I grew to resent and hate her just as much as I did my classmates.

What baffled me the most, though, was the class's unanimous choice of me as the victim. There was another girl in the class who was just as shy and unfriendly as I was. In fact, I don't remember her ever uttering a word. She seemed insecure, and she was plain and not pretty at all. Her personality was unreadable because her face usually wore no expression. However, she did once in a while smile or laugh quietly when the other kids made fun of me.

I was prettier than this girl. I was sure of it. I knew I wasn't ugly anymore, so why were they telling me every day that I was? What was wrong with me that wasn't wrong with this other quiet girl? Why didn't they target *her?*

Well, now I realize there were several reasons. First, her plain looks allowed her to blend in. My looks, though no longer unattractive, were still unusual enough to make me stand out. Second, she was an upperclassman at the below-average math level, like many of the others. I was a studious freshman who got the highest grades in the class. Third, it was true that she acted insecure, but I acted more insecure. Even though I was pretty, I still acted like I was ugly. The years of peer ridicule had damaged me psychologically. I had changed on the outside but not on the inside. I still did not have confidence. Whenever I did try to act self-confident, I think kids viewed it as snobbery because I was so shy and I got straight A's. Of course, the constant abuse in math class made me feel and act more insecure, so the vicious cycle continued.

Looking back on that year, I am amazed and angered at how the kids in that class made me feel so bad about myself and so depressed that I actually longed to die. It's obvious to me now that not one of those kids was better than I was. The boys from the bus and the "Seen the ghost?" guy were all, to be frank, quite lacking in looks and intelligence. As for the rest of them, they were normal enough in looks and intelligence, but like the ringleaders they lacked good character, something much more important.

Which brings me to the next section....

What's Wrong With *Them*

There is always something wrong with the people who are doing the ridiculing. They leave you wondering, "What's wrong with me?" But there is really something more serious that is wrong with them. Often you can figure out part of what's defective in them simply by listening to what they say is defective in you. If they call you ugly, you can bet they're ugly. If they call you stupid, you can bet they're stupid.

Almost all of my attackers were poor students. Hardly any of the boys who made fun of my looks were good-looking themselves. The girls who mocked me were unattractive, plump, or good-looking but poor students. I can say this now because distance from it has made me honest. At the time I was too busy seeing my own faults to pay attention to those in anyone else.

The truth is that everybody has assets and flaws, and everybody is insecure to some degree. But people who ridicule you have something more serious

that is wrong with them: a bad character. They are insecure and seek to feel
better about themselves at your ex-
pense. Maybe you make them feel
threatened and jealous. Or maybe they
aren't threatened by you at all; they
just dislike you, even if they don't
know you and you've never said a
word to them. Sometimes you'll never
figure out their reasons for choosing
you. The point is that they cannot find
their self-worth from within, so they try
to steal it from someone else.

They have a need to put someone else
down to feel good about themselves.
To feel *great* about themselves, in fact.
Seeing someone else get upset and lose
confidence is exhilarating for them, an
emotional high. It makes them feel
powerful and superior. But the sad re-
ality is this: if you get a high out of
hurting someone who has done nothing

to hurt you, it only makes you one
thing—a criminal.

Chapter 3
Enough! How to Stop the Ridicule

If you haven't realized it by now, let me be the one to tell you: unless you pick on others, you *do not* deserve to be picked on. I don't care how you look or how you act. You deserve the same peace, happiness, and security that others enjoy.

Unfortunately, in this world just because you deserve something doesn't mean you'll automatically get it. Sometimes you have to fight for it. I don't mean literally fighting the bullies. I mean taking a serious look at the reasons kids make fun of you and getting rid of as many of those reasons as possible. But before you can become your own self-improvement committee, before you can face the bullies and win, you must first face yourself—and the bullies who may be right there inside you.

What You Can Do on the Inside

In ninth grade I viewed my math class as a daily imprisonment in hell. The door was shut; I could not leave. The teacher was oblivious; I could not depend on her for help. And from the time the bell rang until it rang again, I was forced to stay in my seat while all around me demons jabbed with their pitchforks not at my body but at my tender feelings. Over and over again I was humiliated there. Over and over again I fantasized about defending myself but was held back by fear. (One of the boys from the bus had punched me several times when I was in kindergarten, and I still remembered it.) Even though I was outnumbered, one to a whole class, I never forgave myself for not standing up to the bullies. Gradually two inner demons picked up where the real-life demons left off. Those demons were sadness and anger.

Unfortunately, as in my case, there often seems to be no outlet or relief for the sadness and anger that overwhelm you when you're ridiculed. So you keep your hurt feelings deep inside, where they can wreak havoc on you. The reason they can wreak havoc on you is because, just like wounds to our physical bodies, wounds to our feelings do not simply disappear. When wounds to our feelings are not tended, they can easily become infected, just like physical wounds can. Sadness that becomes infected is depression. Anger that becomes infected is rage.

How much can you accomplish when you're physically sick? Don't you have to get well before you can take care of yourself and do anything productive? Well, when depression has you hating yourself and rage has you hating everybody else, you're about as healthy as someone bedridden with chicken pox and the flu. Whether you're already sick now or just at risk, you need to know how to avoid the emotional infections that ridicule can cause.

Advice on Avoiding Depression

As you go through the changes and
struggles of childhood and adolescence, it's normal for you to doubt
yourself at times, to worry that you
aren't good enough. Then when kids
make fun of you it seems like they're
giving you a terrible answer to your
worst fear: No, you're not good
enough.

Don't believe them!

Whatever you do, don't silently join
the bullies in putting yourself down.
If you are ridiculed often, or if you
doubt yourself to start with, it's easy
for you to agree that you are stupid,
ugly, or whatever garbage the bullies
feed you. Even if they call you Fatso
and it's true that you are overweight,
you start to agree with their real mes-

sage—that you are worthless. In your head you repeat their jeers when they aren't even around. Then you go farther by telling yourself that you're not worth liking or loving and that no one will ever care about you.

This type of thinking is dangerous. It will make you feel more insecure, which will make you act more insecure, which will make kids pick on you more. It could lead you to such despair that you might conclude life is not worth living. Or it could become a bad habit that you carry into adulthood, making yourself miserable long after the bullies are gone.

You must make every effort to stop yourself from thinking self-destructive thoughts that feed depression. Here's one strategy that worked for me. Whenever you start putting yourself down, take a moment to divide yourself into two people: #1, the bully and #2, the person who is being hurt by the bully. Then, as person #2, tell off person #1. If you don't have enough sympathy for the part of you who is person #2, think of someone you care about. Someone vulnerable like a little sister or brother. Someone you know would be hurt if another kid made fun of her or him. How would you feel if a bully were telling this person the hurtful things that you're telling yourself? Wouldn't you want to protect the person? Think of your inner self as that sensitive person you care about, and tell the destructive voice in your head to shut up.

Instead of knocking yourself down, try to comfort yourself. I don't mean to feel sorry for yourself; that doesn't get you anywhere. But there's nothing wrong in feeling sympathy for yourself. It also helps to remember that God loves you. He created you. You are His child, and just like an artist who loves his artwork, He does not take kindly to those who criticize you. Neither do your parents, your siblings, or your real friends.

You may or may not believe in God. You may or may not feel that anyone loves you. You may or may not love yourself. But one thing is certain: you were born for a purpose, and that purpose is *not* to be jeered at by your peers! You are worth more, much more, than that. Please allow yourself to believe in your worth. Let yourself feel good about your strengths instead of focusing on your weaknesses. If you don't think you have any strengths, you are wrong. (For one thing, you have modesty!) Everyone has strengths; it's

just a matter of figuring out what they
are.

There are many ways you can nurture
yourself and many resources out there
to help you do it. If you are inspired
by religion, the Bible can give you
hope, and youth church groups can
link you to quality supportive people. If
it makes you feel better to talk about
your problems, sympathetic ears can be
found. (Keep in mind, though, that you
will need to take a turn listening to the
other person's problems, too, unless the
listener you choose is a paid counselor
or your pet dog.) If you prefer to comfort yourself in solitude, creative outlets such as drawing, singing, and writing can nourish your spirit. Do whatever makes you feel good about yourself, but choose activities that stimulate
personal growth, not stunt it. What I
mean by that is you shouldn't be taking

any drugs unless they are prescribed to you by your doctor.

If you're at the point where no activities have appealed to you for a long time, nothing brings you joy, all you want to do is sleep, or you're always too agitated to sleep, you are probably infected with depression. In that case, you could use the more heavy-duty help of a psychologist or psychiatrist. There is no shame in this; there *is* shame in letting an infection beat you when you could have taken steps to heal it.

No matter what resources you use to help yourself, the most important resource is your own spirit. You have the power to choose between hope and hopelessness. Focus on thoughts that are both realistic and positive. Accept that not everyone will like you and sometimes there will be nothing you can do about it. Accept that some people may dislike you for no apparent reason, even when they don't know you at all.

DO NOT accept that this means you are less of a person.

Advice on Avoiding Rage

It is completely understandable why being ridiculed would make you angry. You are being punished unjustly when you have committed no crime. The bullies are committing a crime, and they're getting away with it—even getting rewarded for it. The adults who witness the crime usually neither stop nor punish the bullies. The kids who witness it, instead of looking down on the bullies for being the nasty jerks that they are, seem to look down on you, labeling you a weirdo, an outcast, a misfit, or a nerd. In short, the bullies get to have fun and feel good about themselves; you get to be stigmatized. It doesn't really make any sense. The ridiculing should make the bullies look bad because their behavior is immature, stupid, cold-hearted, and obnoxious. But, incredibly, it makes *you* look bad! People assume that, if you inspire others to ridicule you, there must be something wrong with you, not the bullies.

This is outrageous nonsense. It's just as warped as thinking that, if you're robbed, you're the one who should go to jail, not the thief. Of course, I could preach on about the injustice of it all, and it might prove therapeutic for me, but it wouldn't do you any good. You know it's a rotten situation. What's important is not the situation; it's how you handle it. Are you going to let the anger fester into rage, turning you into what everyone expects: a misfit with a big chip on your shoulder? Or are you going to control yourself, to channel the anger into something positive, proving to everyone that you are a perfectly normal, worthy person who does not deserve to be insulted?

There are a lot of productive ways to deal with and express your anger. Physical exercise in the form of competitive sports can be a healthy outlet. The sport does not have to be competitive, though. Even walking, jogging, and running by yourself can be very refreshing. For emotional exercise you could join the drama club and vent those overflowing feelings, and get a stage high while you're at it, by acting out a part in a play. Joining school activities will also increase your chances of making friends. No matter how shy you are, it's easier to open up to people when you're part of a team and feel the warm camaraderie.

If you're at the point where no positive outlets appeal to you, where all you want to do is sit and think up ways to get revenge on the bullies or society in general, you are probably infected with rage. Perhaps you're actually considering carrying out one of your schemes. Well, before you possibly ruin your future, hurry to a counselor, psychologist, or psychiatrist. As I said before, there is no shame in seeking help from a doctor. Would you be ashamed to see a doctor if you had an ear infection? You'd just want to get better and get back to normal as soon as possible, right? Anyway, if you want to get even with the bullies, the best way to do that—and to avoid rage—is to stand up for yourself in the first place, just as soon as they pick on you. Defending your dignity can be very gratifying. (That was a quick advertisement for Chapter 4.)

Whatever position you play for a sports team, whatever part you act out for the drama club, in real life do not accept the role of victim or outcast. When you feel persecuted and resent everyone for it, you separate yourself from the oneness you have with humanity. Despite how alienated you may feel, you are part of the human race. It is a misconception that no one has feelings like yours. It is a misconception that you are totally different from everyone else. You are special, valuable, and unique, yes; but you are not the star of a video game in which everyone else is some

sort of monster out to get you. Do not
give in to the "me against the world"
attitude that makes you lose your ability to feel for others, to empathize with
them. There are other people out there
who are hurting. There are people who
have a good character and a kind nature, and I guarantee they live closer to
you than you think.

Find them.

What You Can Do on the Outside

If you skipped over "What You Can
Do on the Inside," please go back and
read it. It's hard to change what's
on the outside until you've changed
what's on the inside. Once you've
turned the negative thoughts into posi-

tive ones, you're well on your way to getting rid of the reasons for people to make fun of you. If you can build up your confidence on the inside, it will give you the courage to make the necessary changes on the outside to improve your social life. Any changes—even if they are positive ones—can be scary to try. The less confidence you have, the more apprehension you will feel at the prospect of trying something new. For example, it's easier and more comfortable to keep the same hairstyle you're used to, even if it looks frumpy. And it's safer and less stressful to continue being shy, even if becoming more outgoing might earn you a new friend.

But think of it this way: Is it better to stay sick or to get well? If you stay sick, life is bad but easy. You sleep and do nothing, lying around in your bed all day. If you get well, life is good but difficult. You feel better, but now you have to do the homework that's piled up, take make-up tests, and deal with all the many pressures that people and life can put on you. But then again, you can also spend time with the people you care about, enjoy your favorite foods, go out to the movies, pursue your dreams, and fall in love.

Wouldn't you rather get well?

Advice on the Way You Look

There are times when we feel it is necessary to change our physical appearance before we can feel and act as confident and outgoing as we would like. There's nothing wrong with that, but don't be unreasonable with yourself. Change what you can and come to terms with what you can't. For example, if your hair is always flat and greasy, you can go to a salon or barbershop and ask for help. Get a new hairstyle and buy some good hair products. If you think you'd look better with earrings, get your ears pierced. (Of course, permission from parents may be required.) If you think you'd look better with muscles, work out. If your clothes are out of style, buy some new ones. (Don't spend too much money on them, though. It's not worth it.) All of these are aspects of your appearance that you can change. However, what if the thing that makes you most depressed about yourself is an aspect of your looks that you cannot change?

First, make sure it is something that cannot be changed. Become informed. Do research at the library or see your doctor. For example, a girl might notice hair growing in places where it should not be growing. It makes her feel hopeless because she thinks there is nothing she can do to fix it. But if she sees her doctor about it, she will find out that 1) she may have a treatable hormonal imbalance causing the problem and 2) she can go to an electrologist to get unwanted hair removed for good.

Drastic plastic surgery, however, like nose jobs, should be out of the question because you are not fully grown yet. (I hope when you are fully grown you will still decide against it.) Also, if you're becoming fanatical about fixing a problem, it is best to seek outside help. When you believe you are overweight, it's okay to cut back on junk foods and do some exercise. It is not okay to starve yourself and run until you drop. Ask a dietitian to help you come up with a healthy plan for losing weight.

So, what if you've done your research and found that there's nothing you can do to change what's bothering you? Well, there is still hope. In a few years nature may solve the problem for you. It did for me! Well, more or less. There are some things about the way I look that I'll never like, and I think that's the way it is with everyone. The funny thing, though, is that some of the features that bother me are the same ones that earn me compliments. Women have always told me how lucky I am to be so thin, but I've always wished for a more shapely figure. The kind of curvy, feminine figure that I envy usually belongs to someone who thinks she's fat. (She isn't, of course.)

DEANNA MILLER

Here I am in middle school—
my awkward years of braces and ridicule.

TIME TO TELL 'EM OFF!

Here I am after I grew.
See how nature (plus a perm) solves the problem for you?

Everyone has a different opinion of what is beautiful. It's all subjective. So don't trick yourself into believing that one of your features is ugly when it's really perfectly fine. We're very good at doing that, you know. If you stare at anything long enough, it can start to look ugly to you, even when it's not. The human brain seems to have a built-in reflex that works like a screen saver in a computer. If you dwell on one feature, one body part, or just your looks in general instead of other aspects of life, your brain gets tired of focusing on the same picture for so long. The screen saver kicks in, and your brain makes the picture shift. It stretches it this way; it smashes it that way; it makes it bigger; it makes it smaller. Before you know it, you're looking at a distortion, but you're still under the impression that it's the original picture. I believe this is what happens to anorexics when they see themselves as fat when they are really bone thin.

The screen saver is your brain's way of telling you: "I'm sick of this subject! Think of something else! Use my powers for good, not evil!" It is wise to trust this message instead of trusting the crazy picture of yourself. Remember that when you worry about the way you look—whether the flaws are real or not—it has a negative effect on something more important: the way you act.

Advice on the Way You Act

Have you ever known people who were good-looking when you first met them but who, after you got to know them, started to look more and more unattractive? Have you ever met people who did not strike you as good-looking at first but who grew more and more attractive as you got to know them? This is the proof that the way you act can change the way you look to others.

Basically, when you don't like yourself and don't like other people, you look worse. When you like yourself and like other people, you look better. You shine. So what it takes to look your best is confidence in yourself and kindness toward others. You may be rolling your eyes at this point because the kids in the popular crowd at your school are anything but kind. Well, the most popular kids tend to be masters at liking themselves and making others admire them, but they are failures at appreciating other people. They act like they're the greatest things to set foot in the school and everyone else is lint between their toes. These kids are not good examples to follow. Why they are so popular and what's so special about them has always been and will always be a mystery to me. I don't care how beautiful they look (which they don't always) or how super-confident they act; if they treat other people badly, they are not special at all. They are like tricky salesmen of worthless wares. They are very good at selling the idea that they are great. But what's inside the pretty box with the bold label? Nothin' but junk!

People at the opposite extreme—those who don't like themselves enough but like others too much—are not good role models either. These are the kids who try so hard to make others like them that they end up annoying every-one. They are too needy, too clingy. They act as if they are begging for friends. Because they give other people too much credit, they don't realize it when people are trying to tell them to get lost. Those with this problem may talk too much, make a big effort to entertain but not be funny, or let themselves be used by other more popular kids.

So, who is a good example of how to act then? Well, in every school—in every grade, really—there are usually a few kids who do not fit in any category. They are not desperately trying to win friends. They do not stick to just one tight circle of friends. They are not nerds, but they are smart. They are not part of the snobby popular groups, but they are on good terms with them. They are not outcasts, but they are on good terms with them, too. And who are these social superheroes? They are genuinely nice people who have the ability to act confident without being snobby and to act friendly without coming off as fake or needy. I do not mean that they are perfect. They aren't. The reason they have such success is because they honestly like themselves, they honestly like people, and it shows. Sometimes they might make you jealous because they seem so happy and they have so much going for them. But they wish nobody ill will, so how can you not like them? These are the people, if any, who should be your role models.

Try to learn by watching these people, but don't expect yourself to become like them right away. Especially if you are used to acting shy, it will be hard for you to start acting friendly. The main thing is to try to be nice. If you're too shy at first to say anything, at least make an effort to smile at people.

Don't wear a sour face. Don't stare all the time at the ceiling or the floor; there are no potential friends there unless you prefer to hang with the bugs.

While it may be hard to become like the social superheroes of your school, it's often easy to befriend them. This is also an excellent way to cut short the ridicule. For example, my problems with ridicule miraculously ended at about the same time I became best friends with one of those all-around nice kids. And I hardly even had to do any work to get the friendship started: it resulted from a lot of effort on her part and a lot of dumb luck on my part. However, it didn't happen until I tried acting more confident and friendly in general.

You may be shy because you're afraid that if you open up to others they will reject you. Believe me, I understand how you feel! But other kids probably do not realize you feel that way. They might assume that the reason you don't look at them or talk to them is because you are stuck up and think you're too good for them. Remember that other people have insecurities, too. Try not to get caught up in yourself too much. Make it a rule to look outward, not just inward. Give yourself and others the benefit of the doubt.

I know, I know—some kids don't deserve the benefit of the doubt. The same rule applies, though, to kids who make fun of you: don't hide inside yourself; look outward and face the criminals!

Chapter 4
Strike Back! How to Defend Yourself

Making positive changes in yourself from the inside out will discourage kids from picking on you. But sometimes that's not enough, especially if they've made a habit of picking on you for a long time. Even if you take away all their reasons for making fun of you, they've still got one reason left: they have a good time being nasty to you. They enjoy the reaction they get from you. They crave the great feeling that comes with putting you down. So, what you need to do now is take the fun out of it for them. Yes, it's time to tell 'em off!

I know it may sound like a scary idea, but it really is necessary at times to defend yourself. I rarely did this because I was afraid two things might happen: 1) the verbal attacks would get worse, or 2) it would lead to physical attacks. I just didn't want the ridicule to get any worse, and I thought it would if I challenged the attackers. But guess what I learned? The ridicule definitely *will* get worse if you do not defend yourself. When people find out they can get away with walking all over you, they don't just walk. They stomp. So, if it's going to get worse anyway, what have you got to lose?

Also, you may not realize it now, but someday when you're an adult and you look back on these days, you'll regret it if you didn't stand up for yourself. You'll wish you'd told off the people who deserved it instead of letting those criminals walk free.

Not defending yourself makes you feel worse about yourself and others. So, start following these rules of self-defense, and see how much better you feel!

Rule #1:
Don't Expect Other People to Stand Up for You

It's nice when other people stand up for you. They save you the trouble of facing the bullies yourself. They make you feel good—or at least less lousy—because you know someone else thinks that the bullies are acting like jerks and that you don't deserve the bad treatment. Unfortunately, as nice as it is, it isn't a permanent solution. The jeering will start up again sometime when your protector isn't around, and it'll be up to you to do the dirty work yourself.

If one of your peers stands up for you, it's okay to thank the person. However, it is not a good idea to try to attach yourself to the person. Your defender may not want to be your friend. You are not on equal footing with people who have the courage to defend you when you do not. Even though they stood up for you, they still may not respect you because you were not able to stand up for yourself. Just take what they did as a sign that others see your worth, and use it as fuel to help you defend yourself the next time.

In general, unless you're in danger of physical harm, don't ask parents, teachers, or counselors to defend you. That works only as long as you're about five years old. Kids will not respect you for turning to adults. The criminals may stop bothering you for a little while if they get in trouble with the principal, but it will certainly start up again, and when it does it'll be worse than ever: "Did you tell your daddy on us? Aw, the poor baby went crying to her daddy...."

Well, you get the picture. By involving adults you've given your attackers big proof that they've hurt you. That's just what they wanted to do, so they love to hear of their success. Hearing it from the principal makes it all the more exciting for them. And all the more humiliating for you.

The best situation is when you know adults you can talk with but trust not to take action themselves. Find adults who can give you both sympathy and good advice.

Rule #2:
Don't Ignore Your Attackers

While kids are making fun of you, one of the worst things you can do is pretend to ignore them in the hopes that they will lose interest and stop. They won't. They know you can hear them, and if you act like you can't, they'll take that as a challenge and keep at you. You may hope that, by ignoring them, you'll make them think that you are not bothered by what they're saying. Even though you do not look at them or speak to them, your nonverbal

71

reactions—clenching your teeth, staring straight ahead, frowning, etc.—give them enough proof that they are upsetting you. That's all the encouragement they need to continue.

Rule #3:
Be Ready to Stand Your Ground

If kids have gotten away with ridiculing you before, they won't back down the first time you defend yourself. When challenged, they'll work harder to put you back in your place. So your defense cannot be halfhearted. You can't throw a punch (not literally, of course) and then expect them to leave you alone as you go hide in the corner again. You've joined the fight, and now they're ready to see it to the end. Brace yourself for the power struggle, and be ready to stand your ground. Don't give up when the ridicule seems to get worse. Remember—it would have gotten worse anyway. This is your chance to make them know that, if they hurt you, you're going to hurt them back.

Do not believe the argument some adults like to use that, if you hurt the bullies back, you're letting them bring you down to their level. Criminals should be stopped. Adults do not meekly tolerate robbers, and neither should you.

Rule #4:
Get Quick With the Comebacks

Your best way of defending yourself is to come up with clever comeback lines for everything rude and nasty they say to you. These comebacks should not be said with a lot of emotion, just a lot of confidence. Make sure you don't mumble the comebacks, either. Speak clearly so they can hear you. Try not to act angry or agitated, and do not make threats of physical violence. Act mildly annoyed, like the bullies are no more bothersome to you than gnats. You don't want to show them they are upsetting you. The purpose of comebacks is to make your attackers look stupid, which really isn't too hard because usually the insults they spit out are stupid.

If you freeze up and can't think of good comebacks right on the spot, don't worry. Just practice at home on your own. Think of some insults they might say and how you can turn their words around to insult them back. Here are some examples:

Insult: "You're so ugly."
Comeback: "You need your eyes checked."

Insult: "You look like a witch."
Comeback: "That's really funny coming from a hag."

Insult: "Don't look at me, loser."
Comeback: "Why? You're not *that* ugly."

Insult: "Would you like a knuckle sandwich?"
Comeback: "No thanks. I'm on a diet."

Insult: "You're so stupid."
Comeback: "So few brain cells. Don't waste them on speech."

Insult: "Look at your metal mouth!"
Comeback: "Look at your crooked teeth!"

Insult: "You're such a skinny freak."
Comeback: "Thanks, Fatso."

Insult: "Hey, Fatso!"
Comeback: "Hey, Big-Nose!"

Insult: "Hi, Four-Eyes!"
Comeback: "They're protective shields for looking at you."

Insult: "What a zit-face!"
Comeback: "At least it doesn't take plastic surgery to fix *my* problem."

No matter what you say, your comebacks will work better if you have already taken steps to be nicer and friendlier with people in general. Then, when you are attacked and you defend yourself, you'll have other kids rooting for you. However, if your supporters encourage you to throw a punch, or if you feel angry enough to start a fistfight, try to control yourself. It's a bad idea to respond to a verbal attack with a physical attack. You should respond in kind. So the opposite is also true: if someone insults you with a physical action instead of a verbal taunt, the comeback is more effective if it is physical instead of verbal. This is an exception to rule #5, but I want to mention it here because it falls under the category of comebacks. The best way to explain it is to give you an example.

My boyfriend J. recently told me a true story of how, when he was in fifth grade, he defended himself after a kid rode by on a bike and spat on him. J. chased the kid and knocked him off his bike. This swift payback was much better than any verbal comeback J. could have yelled at the boy. Anyway, what can you possibly say that would cut someone down to proper size after he spits on you and pedals off? Nothing I can think of! Physical comebacks are more risky than verbal ones, but in J.'s case it worked because the kid never bothered him again.

As you will see in the next section, I generally do not recommend physical violence. However, when exceptions like J.'s arise, I say: let the comeback fit the crime.

Rule #5:
Avoid Physical Fights

Verbal fights made up of insults and comebacks are okay. Physical fights are generally not okay. If it looks like the fight is going to turn physical, avoid the violence any way you can. This might not sound brave, but it's smart. Do you really want to let those idiots get you suspended or expelled? They aren't worth it. Maybe you feel that your pride is worth it, though. Well, there are other ways to save your pride. A few insults are no reason for someone to get beaten up—especially if that someone is you!

This is the difficult part about defending yourself with comebacks. What if it provokes them to attack you physically? Obviously, if you're attacked you have no choice but to fight back in self-defense. However, bullies usually do not attack before first threatening to attack, and sometimes they threaten to attack when they have no real intentions of attacking. So, what do you do if they only threaten physical harm? First, try to figure out if they're bluffing. Have they beaten up kids before? Would it be possible for them to corner you somewhere, like during gym class or while you're walking home from school?

At this point it's a good idea to ask a responsible adult for advice.

If you have any doubt, it's best to ease up on the comebacks for a while until you can feel them out. Your safety should be your priority. That doesn't mean you should act frightened and insecure. Continue to concentrate on acting confident in front of them even if you're worried.

Being officially challenged to a fight is the hardest situation because they'll try to make you look like a coward if you show any sense and do not accept the challenge. You have to find out if the person is just trying to scare you or if he is seriously ready to go through with it. You could try to laugh it off as if he were joking. You could say, "Am I that important to you?" and hope the dummy realizes you are not.

If the bully is serious and you know you could not win, it's better not to fight, even if it sets you back socially. You'll probably be set back socially if you get beaten up, too! If you believe you could win, I don't blame you for fighting, although it should still be your last resort. I personally prefer peace to war. However, some people must be dealt with the same way our government deals with certain hostile foreign governments: talking does no good with them, and the only thing they can understand is a show of force. Before you fight the challenger, though, think about whether it would be a fair fight. Might this person pull out a weapon?

Might his buddies join in, outnumbering you?

Also, keep in mind that beating someone in a fistfight will not necessarily end your problems. It is true that certain kids will avoid messing with you if you win, but certain other kids may want to fight you *because* you won. This is the same "challenger fights the winner" mentality that you see on TV boxing matches, and it's common in schools.

If it is you, not the bully, who is angry enough to start a fight, take a couple deep breaths, get some oxygen to your brain cells, and think. What would you be doing if you threw the first punch? You'd be 1) letting him know he really upset you, 2) inviting possibly more than one person to punch you back, and 3) ensuring that you would be the one the principal would consider at fault because you'd be the one who started the fight.

When physical violence is a possibility, try to prevent the whole mess by taking some classes in self-defense or karate. The idea is not to injure someone. It's just that people are less likely to ridicule and fight you when they know you have a black belt in karate. One guy I know lifted weights and built up his muscles to discourage kids from wanting to fight him. It worked.

A Note on the Rise in Violent Crimes at Schools

I grew up in the suburbs, so the conclusions I've drawn are based on that background. I was not exposed to

83

the dangers of inner-city schools. The worst thing that could happen to you physically at my school was getting beaten up. This was before the unfortunate days of school shootings, the new peril of suburban schools. Whether you're in the city or the suburbs, please use your best judgment in deciding your likelihood of getting chased with a gun in response to your comebacks. If you believe the bully could really be that dangerous, you need to focus on following "What You Can Do on the Outside" in Chapter 3 instead of using comebacks. The whole point of this book is your survival, mentally, emotionally, spiritually—but also physically, the most basic form of all. I want you to *survive* peer ridicule, not lose your life over it.

It is ironic, though, that in every case I've heard of so far, the school shooting has been committed not by the bullies but by their targets. This is a terrible shame. A few kids infected with rage have made society suspicious of all innocent young people who are ridiculed. However, it's a relief to know that bullies do not have a history of going on shooting sprees.

Rule #6:
Kill 'Em With Kindness

I remember an overweight girl who was ridiculed by some other girls on my notorious school bus. Every day when she climbed aboard, she would cast a sour look at her attackers before they even started attacking her. She might as well have said, "Well, here I am! Please make fun of me again!" She had every right to dislike those girls because they had just ridiculed her on the previous bus ride. So it was natural for her to act hostile toward them. I probably did the same thing in my math class without even realizing it. However, it is wiser in these situations *not* to act natural. Do not show your resentment if the bullies have not started attacking you yet. Force yourself to start fresh with each encounter. Be nice and pleasant; act like you do not hold grudges.

I don't mean you should give the bullies a big smile and try to make chitchat with them. I mean you should avoid frowning at them, rolling your eyes, or doing anything to invite them to ridicule you. Then, if they do ridicule you, give it back to them according to rule #4—right then, not the next day, out of the blue, after you've finally thought of a winning comeback line. If you act mean to them anytime other than after they have just insulted you, *you've* now become the criminal! Your job is not to start confrontations; it's to finish them on the spot. Do not bide your time waiting for a chance to get even with the bullies at a moment when they aren't even bothering you. On the contrary, if they aren't ridiculing you, do not interact with them at all unless an opportunity arises where you could do something nice for them.

Yes, that's right: something nice for them.

Now before you toss this book away in disgust, to use it later as a bug-swatter, let me explain the idea of killing 'em with kindness. Actually, there's a quote from the Bible that sums it up better than I could. It goes like this:

If your enemy is hungry, give him food
    to eat;
if he is thirsty, give him water to drink.
In doing this, you will heap burning
    coals on his head,
and the Lord will reward you.

(Proverbs 25: 21, 22)

What does this mean? Well, we all have our own interpretations of the Bible, but to me this means that, when you are kind to people who have been unkind to you, you could make them feel sorry for treating you badly. They could change their minds about you; feel embarrassment, shame, or regret for their bad behavior; and resolve to be nicer to you. On the other hand, when you are mean to people who have been mean to you, you confirm their low opinion of you and make them feel that their nasty behavior was justified.

(Note: Defending yourself with comebacks is *not* the same as being mean!)

There are good approaches and bad approaches to being kind to mean people. Here are some examples of each.

Good approaches:

1) The bully can't find his pencil, so you give him one of yours and tell him to keep it.

2) The bully drops something without noticing, so you pick it up and say, "Here, you dropped this."

Bad approaches:

1) You let the bully copy your homework or look at your answers during a test. When you help someone cheat, you're allowing yourself to

be used, and you're allowing the person to be lazy. So you're not being very nice to yourself or to the other person.

2) You bring a big bag of candy to school and pass it around during class, hoping it will make you more popular. I think this scheme only works if you're a substitute teacher. I've seen an unpopular kid try it, and it didn't help her. Everyone liked her candy, but they still didn't like her.

Use your common sense when deciding how to be nice to a bully. Don't be a sucker. If you let him borrow lunch money from you once and he never pays you back, obviously don't let him borrow from you again.

Chapter 5
When Friends Turn on You

It's natural for friends to tease each other without meaning any harm. Unfortunately, though, it can happen that an argument breaks up a friendship, leaving you stunned to find yourself being ridiculed by the very person who was once your friend.

When your friends start making fun of you, it can be even more painful than when kids you don't know ridicule you. At least when your attackers are strangers you can console yourself by reasoning that they would not be jeering at you if they knew you. But friends do know you. They're supposed to appreciate you and see your worth. They're not supposed to abuse you.

Ex-friends know just how to get to you because at one time you gave them your trust and confided in them. They know things about you that other kids don't. They know better than anyone what your insecurities are and what upsets you the most. So they can easily hurt you.

But guess what? It works both ways! Give ex-friends the benefit of the doubt at first, but if they persist in ridiculing you, give it right back to them. Comebacks are the perfect way to defend yourself against ex-friends because you know what their sore spots are and you can use that knowledge against them, just as they are doing to you. Also, you'll already have a pretty good idea whether they are the types who would get physically violent with you.

Even if you succeed in stopping your ex-friends from picking on you, this is still a sad end to a friendship. Blaming yourself doesn't do much good because sometimes it's just out of your hands. However, here are some steps you can take to decrease the chances that friends will turn on you in the future:

1) This is obvious, but I'll say it anyway: don't make friends with kids who bully others. You can't trust them.

2) Don't make friends with kids who do a lot of gossiping, or talking badly about other people behind their backs. You can't trust them.

3) As I said in "Advice on the Way You Act," try to make friends with the all-around nice people at your school. (Warning: Do not mistake members of the popular, snobby crowd for nice people.)

4) Don't make a habit of talking about other people in a bad way. Nice people won't like you for it.

5) Beware of friendships that are mostly based on cut-downs said jokingly. You know—when someone insults you and then says, "Just kidding!" A friendship like this may help you practice for facing the bullies with comebacks, but if the person hurts your self-esteem, find another friend. There's a reason why people say that every joke has some truth to it. Real friends give each other confidence; they don't put

each other down, even if it's just in fun.

6) Be considerate of your friends' feelings. Always be kind, but do not waste your time trying to sustain friendships with those who are mean to you.

7) Resolve any problems with friends right away before these problems get out of hand. Keep the lines of communication open, apologizing or setting things straight as soon as there is a misunderstanding, before there is time for bad feelings to accumulate and fester.

8) There are times when friends can make all the difference between happiness and sadness, so cherish those who choose to pass their time with you.

Chapter 6
Huh? A Benefit of Being Ridiculed?

I'm just as sick as you probably are of being told that bad experiences will make you a better person. When kids made fun of me, I was not thinking, "Oh, goody! Something to build my character." It felt like my character was being torn down before I could even get the foundation built.

But going through that experience can make you more sensitive to other people's feelings—a quality that definitely is valued in the adult world. You know what it feels like to be discriminated against for no good reason at all. Because you know how awful it feels, and how unjust it is, it should be easy for you to treat everyone with respect, whatever their race, religion, gender, beliefs, etc. You know they are people with feelings, no matter how different they are from you.

Yes, in that way being ridiculed can make you a better person.

Chapter 7
Good Luck!

Here's a brief summary of what to do when kids make fun of you:

1) Try to figure out why they are targeting you. This means taking a look at what they *believe* to be wrong with you while remembering that there is really something wrong with *them*.

2) Take away their reasons for ridiculing you. First, be kind to yourself by replacing negative thoughts with positive ones, avoiding the pitfalls

of depression and rage. Second, fix or come to terms with your physical hang-ups. Third, concentrate on acting confident and friendly.

3) Following the six rules of self-defense, defend yourself without acting upset.

Childhood and adolescence are really a short part of your life, but they seem to last a long time, and their impressions stay with you long afterward. You won't have to live with the bullies all your life, but you will have to live with yourself all your life. So don't let their mocking voices become inner voices of self-hatred and self-doubt that you take with you into adulthood. You are a worthwhile person; don't let any of those idiots convince you otherwise. Stop the criminals now and get on with the happy and successful future that awaits you.

Chapter 8
But What If...?

What if the advice in this book just doesn't work for you, or you find that it's too hard to follow it?

Well, first I want to say that I truly hope my advice helps you improve your situation. I wrote what I believe would have helped me when I was being ridiculed daily and I was so clueless I followed disastrous adult advice like "Just ignore them" and "Don't let them bring you down to their level." If the book doesn't work for you, though, please don't conclude that there's something wrong with you. The last thing I want to do is give you another reason to feel bad about yourself. Blame it on the book!

Second, whether or not you follow anything else you've read here, I want to ask that you please follow the advice on what to do on the inside. The most important thing you can do is treat yourself with kindness, no matter how anyone else treats you. Guard against depression and rage, nurture yourself, believe in yourself, and the rest will eventually follow.

Chapter 9
Additional Resources

Here are some good Web sites that offer help and links to other useful sites.

Sites on bullying:

http://www.cary-memorial.lib.me.us/bullyweb

http://www.teasingvictims.com

http://www.successunlimited.co.uk/bullycide/index.htm

http://www.nobully.org.nz

http://www.scre.ac.uk/bully/index.html

http://www.pleasestop.com/bullying.html

Site on depression:

http://www.geocities.com/pood_72581

Site on rage:

http://members.aol.com/AngriesOut/index.htm

Site with links on just about every possible teenage problem:

http://www.angelfire.com/co/Links4Teens

You can find others by searching the Web with the keywords *bullying, depression*, and *anger*.

About the Author

Deanna Miller has a degree from the school of hard knocks. She was ridiculed so often as a child and teenager that she discovered—the embarrassing way you'd rather not go through—what the causes and solutions are to this problem.

The author also has a B.A. in English with a concentration in language, writing, and rhetoric and a supporting area in business. In addition, she has taken all but one course (because it was always canceled!) required for a technical writing certificate. Having worked as a technical writer, nanny, copy editor, and journal managing editor, she currently copyedits for a weekly newsmagazine.

Also by Deanna Miller:

SKY BOUNCE,

an intermediate/young adult fantasy that was nominated by the late Jean E. Karl for the Pushcart Press Editors' Book Award.

Hesper the Alula and her secret friend Tristan the Boytaur are caught spying on a Sending ceremony, so Hesper is the next Alula who is Sent to the human plane to save the parallel planes from destruction. When Tristan finds her, Hesper must figure out the real solution to the planes' troubles as she struggles with her fear and her tender feelings for the friend who should be her foe.

http://www.geocities.com/deanna_511